LEADERS OF
ANCIENT GREECE

THEMISTOCLES Defender of Greece

THEMISTOCLES Defender of Greece

Ian Macgregor Morris

rosen
central

Published in 2004 by The Rosen Publishing Group, Inc.
29 East 21st Street, New York, NY 10010

First Edition

Library of Congress Cataloging-in-Publication Data

Morris, Ian Macgregor.
Themistocles: defender of Greece / Ian Macgregor Morris.
     p. cm. — (Leaders of ancient Greece)
Includes bibliographical references and index.
ISBN 0-8239-3830-1
1. Themistocles, ca. 524–ca. 459 B.C. 2. Greece—History—
Persian Wars, 500–449 B.C. 3. Greece—History—Athenian
supremacy, 479–431 B.C. 4. Statesmen—Greece—Biography.
5. Generals—Greece—Biography. I. Title. II. Series.
DF226.T45 M67 2003
938'.03'092—dc21

                                            2002007367

Manufactured in the United States of America

CONTENTS

GREECE AT THE TIME OF THEMISTOCLES

BLACK SEA

MACEDONIA

THRACE

• Sigeum

• Acanthus

AEGEAN SEA

• Phocaea

• Ephesus

Chalcis

Thebes • • Eritrea

Delphi •

• Athens

• Miletus

• Corinth

PELOPONNESE

• Halicarnassus

Olympia Argos

• Sparta

IONIAN SEA

CRETE

MEDITERRANEAN SEA

INTRODUCTION

Greece at the time of Themistocles, from about 525 BC to 460 BC, was a divided place. The Greeks had no concept of nation or nationality and lived in small separate cities, each fiercely independent. No sense of unity existed between them. Most Greeks would much rather have allied with a foreign power than with their neighboring Greek cities. The Greeks called their cities *poleis* (singular: *polis*). The polis was a political community composed of the citizens themselves. To the Greeks, any other form of state, such as the great monarchies that the Greeks observed in the Near East, was a form of tyranny in which people were not free.

The polis was always relatively small. A large polis, such as Athens, had less than 30,000 citizens, but most poleis had only a few hundred. This gave the individuals

The facade of the
Parthenon today

within a polis a considerable amount of freedom and influence in running their city. However, the poleis viewed one another with suspicion, so when a powerful enemy threatened, there was little hope of a defensive alliance. Indeed, when the Persians invaded in 480 BC, many of the Greek poleis actually joined the Persian side. The price of such freedom was great instability.

Ancient Athens lay on the eastern coast of Greece. The Athenians controlled an area of land called Attica, but this was not large enough to supply all their needs, and they became increasingly dependent on foreign grain. This dependence on trade made them an outward looking people, open to new ideas and eager to involve themselves in the world at large. By the time of the birth of Themistocles, Athens was rapidly becoming an important city, and fundamental changes were taking place. Themistocles witnessed both the birth of democracy in Athens and the rise of the greatest threat the Greek cities ever faced—the Persian Empire. He would play a major role in these events.

Before the story of Themistocles can be told, it is important to consider who recorded it. The most important sources for his life story are the *Histories* of Herodotus, who was born c. 485 BC when Themistocles was forty years old and just reaching the pinnacle of his career. Herodotus tells of the great wars between the Greeks and the Persians and the pivotal role that Themistocles played in them. Later writers add many details about his life. Of these, the most important is Plutarch, who wrote a biography of Themistocles. Plutarch lived during the second century AD, 600 years after Themistocles died. Plutarch's account is based on many other sources that no longer survive. Thus, although Plutarch lived a long time after Themistocles, he still preserved many details that would otherwise be lost today.

Many people have seen moral lessons in the rise and fall of Themistocles. However one views him, one cannot deny that he was one of the most important men of his generation. He became a legend in his own lifetime, but he lived to see that legend tarnished and then crumble. His main legacy was not his reputation, however, but the city he left behind. By the time Themistocles died, Athens was the greatest city in Greece and was entering a golden age.

Citizen of Athens

Themistocles of Athens was born in about the year 525 BC, the son of a man named Neocles. Little is known about Themistocles' family. Although they had connections to the aristocracy, they were an ordinary family themselves.

Like all young Athenian males, Themistocles was educated in the skills necessary to be a citizen and a soldier. He learned athletics, competing against other boys in long- and short-distance running, jumping, throwing the javelin and discus, boxing, and wrestling. He was also taught the artistic skills for which the Athenians were so well known, the playing of the lyre, singing, and dancing. But he had little time for these subjects and considered them a pointless distraction. The historian Plutarch notes that from an early age, Themistocles displayed a desire to succeed in politics. His favorite subject was rhetoric, the skill of making speeches, of putting together arguments that would convince his listeners. While the other children played, he practiced the skills that would serve him in politics. He would compose speeches, which he would give in imaginary court cases, defending and prosecuting the other children for imaginary crimes. His teachers noticed this behavior. One of them predicted that Themistocles would grow to be a man of great importance, but he could not tell whether this would be for good or evil.

A young man's education was considered complete when he reached the age of nineteen. At this time, he was brought before the assembly of his *deme*, or local council, and accepted into the community of citizens. As a full citizen of Athens, he was entitled to attend the public assembly, participate in the political life of the city, and serve in the army. But even as Themistocles was reaching the age of citizenship, Athens was undergoing the greatest crisis in its history—a desperate struggle for leadership between the most powerful men of the day, a struggle that would see the birth of the very first democracy in the world.

Athens, like the majority of Greek cities, began existence as a monarchy. By the eighth

A bust of the Athenian statesman and naval commander Themistocles

century BC, the office of the king had been replaced by three elected officials called *archons;* soon afterward, the number of archons was increased to nine. At first, archons served for ten years. Later, they held office for only one year, after which they became members of the Areopagus, a council that advised the archons and oversaw court cases. However, because the Areopagus was composed of former archons, it tended to dominate the government. Also, because all the archons were aristocrats, the government was in the control of the aristocracy. Their control of Athens caused increasing unrest among the rest of the population. By the beginning of the sixth century BC, many of the poorest Athenians had been forced into a form of serfdom, and if they were unable to pay their debts, they were forced into slavery. The situation had become so serious that even the aristocrats realized that something had to change. A man named Solon was appointed to reform the system. Solon reduced the power of the aristocrats and gave rights to the people.

A generation after the reforms of Solon, Athens was still unstable. In 561 BC, a former archon named Peisistratus seized power and proclaimed himself tyrant. To the ancient Greeks, a tyrant was not necessarily a bad ruler. It simply meant a ruler who seized power and ruled without a constitution. In the seventh and sixth centuries BC, many Greek cities were taken over by tyrants, who used the support of the poor to counter the power of the aristocracy. In this way, the traditional aristo- crats' hold on power was loosened, paving the way for the democracies that would follow.

Although twice driven out by his oppo- nents, Peisistratus always managed to return triumphantly, and he ruled Athens until his death in 527 BC. He maintained many of the reforms of Solon and encouraged the Athenians to develop a sense of civic identity. While Peisistratus's rule was a benign one, the rule of his son who succeeded him was not. Hippias became tyrant of Athens upon his father's death, and although he was popular at first, his rule became very harsh. In 514 BC, Hippias's

A terra-cotta sculpture of four bakers kneading dough to the accompaniment of a flute player

brother, Hipparchus, was murdered in a personal dispute. The assassins had also intended to kill Hippias but failed. Still, Hippias became worried that others would try again. Opposition to his rule grew, led by the Alcmaeonids, the most powerful aristocratic family in Athens. In 510 BC, with the help of the Spartans, Hippias was driven out of Athens and fled to Persia.

After the exile of Hippias, various groups of aristocrats competed for control of the city. The young Themistocles may have heard the speeches of these men and watched with fascination as they vied for power. Eventually, one of these leaders, Cleisthenes, realized that the path to power lay in the hands of the ordinary citizens. With the support of the people, Cleisthenes passed a series of sweeping democratic reforms.

Cleisthenes divided the population into ten *phylai*, or tribes. Each tribe would send fifty representatives to the *boule*, a city council. The representatives were chosen by lot and would be members of the boule for only one year. These precautions ensured that no individual could dominate the system by securing his own election and remaining on the council for as long as he wished. However, the boule was not the center of power in the new Athens. The boule merely prepared business for the public assembly, or *ecclesia*. The assembly had existed for many centuries, but it was only under Cleisthenes that it became the most powerful part of the Athenian government. The assembly debated every proposed law and decided all questions of government policy, from the creation of treaties to the declaration of war. Every male citizen over the age of eighteen could attend. No matter how poor or uneducated, every male citizen could speak in the debates and vote on the laws. The Athenian

A painting from the inside of a vase showing a music lesson. A pupil is learning to play the lyre.

assembly was like a congress or parliament, except that instead of being composed of the representatives of the people, it was composed of the people themselves. If Athens was to go to war, it was the men who were to fight in that war, and not their representatives, who made the decision. The Athenian people, or *demos*, now ruled themselves. The first democracy was born.

It was in this new democracy that Themistocles began his career. Although participation in the government was open to all men, the wealthy still had an advantage. Only the rich could afford the education that taught the

Another vase painting of a music lesson. Here, the pupil learns to play the aulos.

skills a politician needed to succeed. And only the rich had the financial backing to devote themselves entirely to politics, without having to earn an income. Although Themistocles was not an aristocrat, he was well educated and probably spent his early years making a name for himself in the debates of the assembly. However, the assembly could be fickle in its decisions. In 499 BC, the assembly made a decision that would carry fearful consequences for the Athenians.

The situation began when an ambassador from the city of Miletus in Asia Minor (modern-day Turkey) arrived in Athens and asked to speak to the assembly. Although the people in the cities along the coast of Asia Minor, known as Ionia, were Greek, they had been under the control of the mighty Persian Empire for fifty years. The Persian Empire encompassed a vast area stretching from the Aegean Sea all the way to India. It stood as the sole superpower of the ancient world. The ambassador, named Aristagoras, wanted the Athenians to help the Ionian Greeks in a revolt against the Persians. He had already visited Sparta, the most powerful of all the Greek cities, but the people had refused to help him. So he came to Athens to ask for help. He described the vast wealth of Persia and the rewards the Athenians could expect for helping the Ionians. He also reminded the Athenians that they were kinsmen. The Greeks traditionally divided themselves into three ethnic groups: the Dorians, Aeolians, and Ionians. The Athenians were considered Ionian, and so the Ionians in Asia Minor, according to Aristagoras, were their brothers.

This argument won over the Athenians, and, not fully considering the potential consequences, the people voted to help the Ionians. Twenty ships were dispatched, each capable of carrying 200 men. This was a significant portion of the Athenian fleet. The Athenians took

A relief carving of Darius I, king of Persia from 550 BC to 486 BC

part in the early stages of the revolt, helping the Ionians capture and burn the city of Sardis, the capital of the western part of the Persian Empire. The news of the sack of Sardis was relayed to Darius, the king of Persia, in his capital of Susa on the Persian Gulf. The historian Herodotus wrote that upon hearing that Sardis had been destroyed, Darius called his advisers to him. "The Ionians," he said, "do not matter. They will be punished in due course. But who are these Athenians? And why do they attack me?" The Athenians had brought themselves to the notice of the Persian king.

The Ionian revolt lasted until 494 BC, when the last rebels were defeated by the Persians. The Athenians, however, withdrew their support after the sack of Sardis. It was during these years that Themistocles rose to prominence in Athenian politics. Little is known of his early career, but in 493 BC he was elected archon. The brush with Persia had a lasting effect on Themistocles. He began pursuing a policy that would underlie his entire political career. The key to Athens's power, he believed, lay at sea. While serving as archon, he drew up plans for the fortification of the Piraeus, a seaport that lay some four miles southwest of the city of Athens. Others, however, did not share Themistocles' view of Athenian naval potential. The Greek city-states were built on the ideal of the warrior-citizen. Each free adult male was also a potential *hoplite*, a soldier trained to wear the heavy bronze armor of the Greek infantryman. The armor of the hoplite was expensive, and it became a status symbol. Those who could not afford the armor had to serve in the army as light infantry, while the poorest citizens had to serve in the navy as rowers. Themistocles' belief in the navy as the strength of Athens went against the very social

An artist's reconstruction of the ship-building sheds discovered at one of Athen's harbors

fabric of Athens. No Athenian hoplite wished to lay down his armor to serve on a ship. Among the opponents of his policy was General Miltiades, who believed that the strength of Athens lay, as it did for every Greek city, in its army. While the Athenians debated, however, the Persians began to march.

With the Ionians defeated, Darius turned toward Greece. At first, he sent his son-in-law Mardonius with an army into Thrace, in what is now the Balkans. The Persians met with heavy resistance, and Darius decided to attack Greece by sea. Ambassadors were sent to the Greek cities to demand "earth and water," the symbols of submission. Many cities submitted, but two refused. The Spartans, long famed for their direct manner, threw the ambassadors down a well with the words: "You will find your earth and water down there!" The Athenians threw the ambassadors into a pit reserved for condemned criminals. The murder of the Persian ambassadors broke every law and custom on the treatment of ambassadors. War with Persia was inevitable.

Darius prepared a fleet to punish the Greek cities that had aided the Ionians. The fleet finally set sail in 490 BC. The historian Herodotus estimated that the Persian fleet consisted of 600 ships, and although this is probably an exaggeration, the navy would still have been large enough to destroy Athens. The Persian army was commanded by General Datis. Hippias, the former tyrant of Athens, who had been driven into exile more than twenty years earlier, accompanied Datis. Hippias hoped to reclaim his position in Athens with the help of Persian arms.

The fleet sailed across the Aegean Sea, conquering many Greek islands on the way. It landed near the city of Eretria, which had also supported the Ionian revolt. The city was besieged, and after a week of bitter fighting, it was taken. In revenge for the destruction of Sardis, Eretria was burned to the ground and the surviving inhabitants sold into slavery. Then the Persians set sail for Athens.

Rather than land near the city itself, the Persians landed at the plain of Marathon, some twenty-six miles to the northwest. It was here, Hippias informed the Persians, that they could best use their cavalry. Upon hearing this news, an Athenian army of only 9,000 men hurried out to meet them. A runner named Pheidippides was sent to Sparta, some 150 miles to the south, where he arrived the following day. He asked the Spartans, famed as the best soldiers in all Greece, to come to the aid of Athens. The Spartans, however, were in the midst of a religious festival and could not march for several days. Pheidippides ran back to Athens and relayed the news. Athens would fight alone. Then, exhausted from his efforts, Pheidippides died. One ally, however, did not fail Athens. The small city of Plataea sent 1,000 men to reinforce the Athenians. So the Greek army at Marathon numbered 10,000 men. They faced nearly 30,000 Persians.

When Cleisthenes designed the Athenian constitution, he had been well aware of the power that a military commander could wield in politics. To prevent any one commander from becoming too powerful, he decided that each of the ten *phyle* would elect one general every year. These men were under the overall

A relief carving showing Scythians and Ionians bringing tribute to Darius I, king of Persia

command of the *polemarch*, or war archon. Thus, when the Athenian army marched to Marathon, they were commanded by ten generals and one polemarch, named Callimachus. Once they arrived and saw the size of the Persian army, the generals argued over what they should do. Half of them feared taking on the Persians in battle. Not only were they outnumbered, they believed that the Persians were better soldiers. During the previous 100 years, the Persians had risen from being a subject people in the empire of the Medes to becoming masters of the Middle East. They had conquered the Medes, the Babylonians, the Egyptians, and a host of other great peoples. So great was the power of the king of Persia that even the Greeks referred to him simply as "The Great King." What hope, asked some of the Athenian generals, could they have against him? Other generals, however, were more determined. They were led by Miltiades, one of the most influential political figures of his generation. He was supported by a young general named Aristides. Miltiades and Aristides convinced Callimachus that the only alternative to fighting the Persians was defeat and slavery. So the decision was made. Athens would fight.

For several days, the two armies faced each other. Finally Miltiades drew up the Greeks for battle. After the preliminary sacrifices to the gods had been made, the Greeks advanced toward the Persians at a run. The Persians, stationed a mile away, could not believe that the Greeks would dare to attack them with so few men. The two armies clashed, and the battle raged long and hard. In order to make his front line as long as that of the Persians, Miltiades had made the center of his line only a few ranks deep; the Persians began to gain the upper hand in the thin center. It was here that Themistocles fought alongside Aristides. The historian Plutarch recorded how they bravely tried to hold the line. But the Persians were too numerous, and the Athenian line began to break. On the flanks, however, the Greeks were having greater success, and eventually the Persian line collapsed. The outer edges of the Greek line curled toward the center. The Persians stationed there, who had sensed victory,

Greek hoplites, infantrymen, putting on their armor

suddenly found them-selves surrounded, and panic set in. The entire Persian line began to break. The Greeks surged forward on all sides, cutting down the fleeing invaders. The Persians tried to retreat to their ships but found their way blocked by their own comrades. As the dust began to clear from the field, the scale of the carnage became clear. The historian Herodotus no doubt exaggerated, but his figures reflect the scale of the victory. More than 6,400 Persians lay dead, as opposed to 192 Athenians.

The surviving Persians, having reached their ships, gazed back at the plain of Marathon in disbelief. They still numbered some 20,000 men, and the entire Athenian army was standing exhausted on the battlefield, twenty-six miles from Athens. Hurriedly the Persians raised their sails and set out for Athens, which was undefended. If the Persian fleet could sail around the peninsula to Athens before the Athenian army could return home, then the Persians might still achieve a victory.

Standing on the battlefield, the Athenians watched the Persians depart with a feeling of dread. Leaving a few men at Marathon to guard the prisoners and tend to the wounded, Miltiades led the army back to Athens. Weary from hours of battle, the Athenians had to run twenty-six miles over the mountains of Attica. In the searing heat of the Greek summer, each man carrying sixty pounds of heavy armor, the army hurried to Athens. As the Persian fleet pulled into view of Athens, they saw the Greek army standing along the cliffs, their shields reflecting the light of the setting sun. Athens was saved.

In the aftermath of the victory, Miltiades was praised as the savior of Athens. Those who had fallen, including the polemarch Callimachus, were buried on the battlefield and worshiped as heroes. Those who had survived strode proudly through the streets of Athens and came to consider the Battle of Marathon as the greatest event of their lives. The poet and playwright Aeschylus, who was admired as the greatest writer Athens ever produced, wanted only one thing mentioned on his tombstone, that he had fought at Marathon.

In the celebrations that followed the victory, one person remained quiet. He did not attend the drinking parties, and he could not sleep at night. When someone asked him why he did not join the celebrations, Themistocles answered sadly, "The poor Athenians. They think the victory of Miltiades is the *end* of the war. Do they not realize, this is just the *beginning*!"

LEADER OF ATHENS

The years between the Battle of Marathon and the second Persian invasion of Greece in 480 BC were filled with great change. The reputation of Athens among the other Greek cities rose steadily. The Spartans had sent a force of 2,000 men to reinforce the Athenians at Marathon, and although they arrived several days after the battle, they still insisted on marching to Marathon to view the results of the Athenian victory. The compliments the Spartans paid to the Athenians were high praise indeed. The Spartans were the foremost experts in the art of war in all of Greece.

In 487 BC, a significant change took place in Athenian politics. A law was passed declaring that the archons, who had been elected, would now be chosen by lot. The idea of selection by lot instead of election was not uncommon in Greek politics. In fact, many believed that it was a fairer form of selection. In elections, the people tended to vote for the most eloquent and charismatic speakers, which usually meant the rich professional politicians. Selection by lot was random, and so anyone could become archon. The usual problems that made elections unfair, such as bribery and intimidation, were no longer an issue, and the hold of the professional politicians on the reins of power was, in theory, broken.

However, the people behind the new law had a hidden agenda. A few positions in the state were still decided by popular election, such as the polemarch and the generals of the army. These were posts that would never be selected by lot. The Athenians could not afford to have just anyone commanding the army. The generals needed to be trained, experienced, and competent leaders, for defeat in war could mean the destruction of the city. For this reason, the position of general was one that could be held more than once.

The selection of archons, however, raised a problem for ambitious politicians such as Themistocles. Once they had held the post of archon, they could not hold it again. Although

An artist's reconstruction of the Painted Stoa, a meeting place on the northern side of the agora, or central market, of Athens

they became members of the Areopagus, which was an important council, they could never again hold the reins of power. Hence, their influence on policy would remain limited. By passing a law that made the selection of archons a matter of chance, the office became insignificant. In the days before the Battle of Marathon, Miltiades had shown how influential the generals could be, and thus the post of general became the most important office in the state. The fact that the rank of general could be held year after year meant that ambitious politicians could remain in office for long periods of time, thus controlling the policy of the state. It is not known who was behind this law, but it is likely that it was Themistocles and other ambitious men like him. He had already served as the archon, and therefore had much to gain from the new system.

In the same year, another major development occurred. The Athenians had a curious ritual in their constitution called ostracism. Each year the people would vote on whether to exile one of the citizens. The person in question need not have committed any crime. The people would gather and cast their votes for the person they wished to see exiled from the city. As long as at least 6,000 people voted, then the person with the most votes would have to leave the city for ten years. During the exile, his property was looked after, and in ten years he could return. There was no disgrace attached to being ostracized. The idea was simply to prevent any one person from becoming too powerful, and thus becoming a tyrant. However, in practice, the ritual was open to corruption, and it was used by leading political figures to dispose of their opponents. The people cast their votes by writing the name of the person they wanted ostracized on a piece of broken pottery. These pieces were then collected and counted. Archaeologists, however, have found large numbers of

A relief carving from the palace of Darius at Susa showing two Persian archers

these pieces written in the same handwriting. This indicates that some people produced large numbers of these pieces with the same name on them and then handed them in to be counted. Many of the poorer Athenians were illiterate and could easily be convinced, often with a bribe, to hand the shards of pottery to the officials, pretending that they had written the names themselves.

It is not known when the ritual of ostracism first appeared in Athens. It may have been part of the reforms introduced by Cleisthenes in 507 BC, or it may have been introduced in 487 BC along with the law on the election of archons. Whatever the case, no one was ostracized until 487 BC. In that year, a man named Hipparchus was ostracized. His name suggests that he was a relation of the former tyrant Hippias, whose brother, also called Hipparchus, was murdered in 514 BC. This Hipparchus was the leader of a faction in Athens that was sympathetic to Hippias, and as such was considered an enemy of the democracy. It would not have been difficult for Themistocles and his allies to rouse the anger of the people against Hipparchus, especially since it was known that Hippias had accompanied the Persians at Marathon. In the years that followed, more people who were

An artist's reconstruction of the Sacred Gate on the Sacred Way, one of the main avenues of Athens

perceived to be sympathetic to Hippias were ostracized, and from 487 BC, someone was ostracized nearly every year. Political life in Athens had suddenly become much more dangerous.

The developments of 487 BC reveal a ruthlessness that had not been present in Athenian politics before. Behind this was the

figure of Themistocles. The increase in the political power of the generals provided such men with the opportunity to hold the most important office in the state year after year, while ostracism was a weapon that could be used to dispose of opponents. Themistocles had displayed a fervent ambition to be the most powerful man in Athens. However, others were aware of his ambition and set out to oppose him. Among them was a young and highly respected politician who had made his name at Marathon, Aristides.

Plutarch provides many examples of the rivalry between Aristides and Themistocles. Most of them are probably fictitious stories invented later on to embellish the legend of Themistocles. However, they do reflect a historical truth—that Themistocles and Aristides were bitter rivals in both public and private

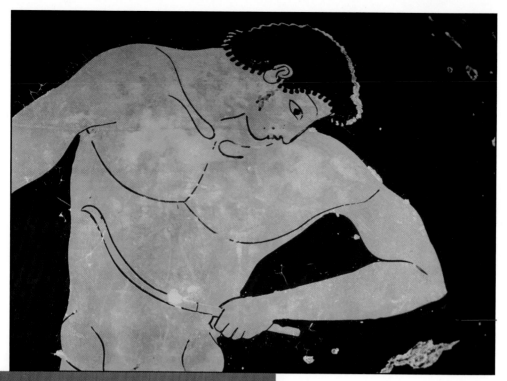

A painting of a Greek youth cleaning his body with an iron scraper. The actual instrument is shown on the bottom.

life. They would block each other's laws, not because the laws were bad, but because of personal enmity. Plutarch describes the characters of the two men as diametrically opposite. Whereas Themistocles was unprincipled, ruthless, and impetuous, Aristides was stable, trustworthy, and virtuous. Indeed, so good was his reputation that people began to call him "Aristides the Just."

Although Themistocles was unscrupulous, he did have a vision. Unlike the majority of Athenians, he believed that the Persian threat had not disappeared. The only hope Athens had, he believed, lay at sea. As early as 493 BC, he had tried to impress upon the Athenians the idea that naval power was the key to their security. This one belief underlay all his policies. In 483 BC, he saw his chance to make his dream a reality.

To the southeast of Attica, at a place called Laurium, lay a complex of silver mines. Worked by slaves who spent much of their lives down in the shafts deep inside the mountains, these mines were an important source of income for Athens. In 483 BC, the miners discovered a rich vein of silver. This new-found wealth yielded a great surplus in the Athenian treasury. When such a surplus appeared, the Athenians usually voted to distribute the money equally among all the citizens. This would have meant a payout of about ten drachma, equivalent to ten days wages, for every citizen. However, Themistocles went before the people and urged them to vote against such a distribution. He knew that he could not convince the Athenians on the basis of the Persian threat. Too few people believed that the Persians would return. However,

A relief carving showing young Athenians playing a ball game similar to hockey

Athens was at war with the city of Aegina at the time. Athens and Aegina had been bitter rivals for many years, and the Athenians had accused them of being sympathetic to the Persians in 490 BC. Moreover, being an island, Aegina had a powerful fleet, the largest in Greece at the time. Themistocles, rather than warn the Athenians about the Persians, concentrated on the rivalry with Aegina. The Athenians' bitter hatred for the Aeginetans was strong enough to make them

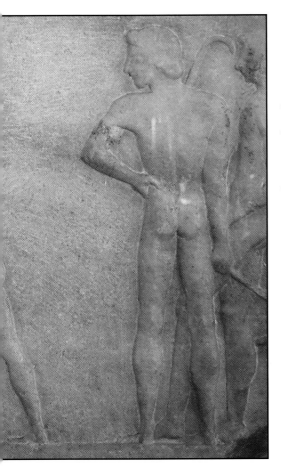

forego the opportunity to take the money for themselves. Themistocles managed to convince the people to spend the money on building a fleet.

The money was used to build 100 *triremes*. The trireme was the standard Greek warship of the time. The trireme was so called because it was powered by three rows of oars on each side, pulled by oarsmen sitting within the hull of the vessel. Each ship was only about 120 feet in length and 20 feet wide, but carried 200 oarsmen. Although the trireme carried a mast and a sail, these were used only for long journeys. In battle, the mast was removed to make the ship more maneuverable. Its main weapon was a bronze battering ram at the bow that was used to crush the hulls of enemy ships. The oarsmen, when highly trained, could turn the ship and propel it forward or backward at great speed. It could ram into an enemy vessel and then withdraw as the other ship sank. Some triremes even carried a small detachment of heavily

armored infantry or a squad of archers who could board and capture enemy ships once they had been rammed, or pepper them with arrows from afar. These weapons, argued Themistocles, could save Athens.

However, some of Themistocles' opponents still tried to stop him; among these opponents was Aristides. Themistocles realized that he could not continue with his polices until he disposed of his opponent. And so he set about having Aristides ostracized. He spread stories that Aristides was secretly trying to become tyrant of Athens. The very word "tyrant" was enough to inflame the passions of the Athenians.

Themistocles also worked on the increasing jealousy that people felt toward Aristides for his pure and faultless reputation.

And so Aristides the Just was ostracized from Athens. Themistocles had proved himself the most ruthless politician in Athens in his attempt to become the most powerful man in the city. Later events would tell whether he was the most capable.

SAVIOR OF ATHENS

CHAPTER 3

In 485 BC, Darius, the king of Persia, died. Xerxes, his son, became the new king. As a young man, Xerxes had seen his father's anger at the Athenian attack on Sardis and had listened in horror of the humiliation at Marathon. As a son, Xerxes felt the duty to fulfill his father's dying wish—to destroy Athens, burn its temples as the Greeks had burned the temples of Sardis, enslave its people, and wipe its very name from the face of the earth. Messengers were sent to every corner of Xerxes' realm with the order to assemble for battle. The great king was preparing for war.

After five years of preparation, Xerxes' army gathered at Sardis. Men from forty-six nations stood beneath Xerxes' banner, each commanded by generals who were kings in their own right.

Egyptians and Babylonians, Scythians and Medes, Indians and Ionian Greeks, all gathered for the march on Greece. Herodotus estimated that the army totaled more than 5 million men and 1,200 ships of war. This is likely to be another exaggeration. Modern estimates place Xerxes' army at about 200,000.

From Sardis, Xerxes sent emissaries to the city-states of the Greek world, as his father had done ten years before, to demand earth and water as symbols of submission. However, Xerxes remembered what had happened to the Persian ambassadors at Athens and Sparta, and so none were sent to these two cities. They could expect no mercy.

The Spartans were the first to know of Xerxes' intentions. They were informed via a secret message sent from an exile who had sought shelter at Xerxes' court. They quickly informed the other Greeks states, and a council was called of those Greek cities willing to resist the invaders. Of the hundreds of cities in Greece, only thirty-one attended. In addition to Athens and Sparta, attendees included Corinth, where the conference was held; Plataea, an old ally of Athens; Aegina, whom the Athenians had once accused of supporting the Persians; and little Thespiae. Conspicuous by their absence were Argos and Thebes, powerful cities that appeared to favor the invaders. Those who showed support for Xerxes even before he arrived hoped that he would reward them after his victory.

At the council, the delegates debated where and how they should resist the enemy. The key to Greek success, Themistocles realized, was unity. Only if the Greek city-states worked together would they have any chance of defeating the Persians. The differences that existed between the cities at the council, such as those between Athens and Aegina, were quickly settled. Ambassadors were sent to the Greek cities that had not attended, in the hope of enlisting their support. It was decided that an army would be sent to the Pass of Tempe in northern Greece to face Xerxes. Under the joint command of a Spartan general and Themistocles, 10,000 men were sent to Tempe. Upon arriving there, they discovered that the pass was indefensible. The army had no option but to withdraw, and the leaders returned to the council at Corinth to decide again where they should resist Xerxes. Before Xerxes had even set foot in Europe, the Greeks were forced to abandon northern Greece to the invaders.

In the meantime, each of the cities sent envoys to the Oracle at Delphi to consult the gods about what they should do. The Athenians approached the priestess (or oracle), through whom they believed the god Apollo spoke. The words of the priestess were not comforting. She told them to flee and that the Persians would lay waste to their city. Disturbed by this prophecy, the envoys asked again if there was anything they could do. The priestess's response was in verse:

> O, Sons of Athens, your city will fall!
> Place your trust in only the Wooden Wall.
> For once you have placed all your faith
>   in this,
> Then Death will smile at Divine Salamis.

With this mysterious prophecy, they returned to Athens. People could not agree about what it meant. Some argued that the "Wooden Wall" referred to the walls of the Acropolis, the sacred hill at the center of the city, because its walls were wooden. The reference to Salamis, an island off the coast, was seen as a warning to avoid fighting the Persians there. However, others, including Themistocles, rejected these interpretations. He asserted that the reference to Salamis as "Divine" proved that it would be the site of an Athenian victory, and it was the Persians upon whom death would smile. Surely, he argued, if the verse was referring to the Athenians, then the oracle would have described Salamis as "hateful," not "divine." As to the "Wooden Wall," the prophecy here was clear. It did not refer to the wall that surrounded the temples on the Acropolis. It referred to the newly built fleet. The navy would be the Wooden Wall of Athens. Themistocles' interpretation convinced the people, who were now willing to place their trust in the fleet.

The Greeks decided to defend their country at a place called Thermopylae, where the road from northern Greece passed between the mountains and the sea. At its narrowest point, this pass was barely wide enough for two carts to pass one another. Here, the Greeks hoped, a small force could hold the vast army of Xerxes, because the Persians would be able to bring only a small fraction of their army into action at any one time. Meanwhile, the Greek navy would defend a place called Artemisium, just to the north of Thermopylae. Again, the narrow channel there would make the superior numbers of the Persian fleet useless. If the Greeks could hold these positions long enough, then the Persian army would begin to experience supply problems. Then, other Greek cities that were remaining neutral would realize that the Persians were not invincible and might join the alliance.

It was decided that the army at Thermopylae would be commanded by Leonidas, king of Sparta. Many in the alliance, however, suspected that the Spartans were not fully committed to defending Greece. The southern half of Greece, called the Peloponnese, was linked to the rest of the country by the Isthmus of Corinth, a thin strip of land to the southwest of Athens. Traditionally, the Peloponnesians had seen this as the natural border to their homeland, and thus, it appeared that some among them wished to make this their line of defense against the Persians. This would leave the cities of central and northern Greece to the Persians. Without the elite armies of Sparta, the Greeks to the north of the isthmus had little hope. For the Peloponnesians, this was of little importance.

The Spartans were formidable soldiers but had little understanding of the potential of naval power. Defending the Isthmus of Corinth

A sculpture of the Spartan commander Leonidas, who died at Thermopylae

would prove fruitless. The Persians could simply use their navy to bypass the fortifications and land troops at any point on the coast of the Peloponnese. The only hope to counter Persian naval power lay with the newly constructed navy of Athens. If the Spartans chose to defend the isthmus, then the Athenians would have no choice but to surrender to Xerxes, and the Persian navy could sail unopposed. Leonidas was one of the few Spartans who understood the vital role the Athenian navy would have to play, and he saw the need to send troops north of the isthmus. The need for unity among the members of the Greek alliance was essential. The Spartans needed the Athenians, and the Athenians needed the Spartans. If Sparta, the greatest of the Greek states, did not lead the united resistance, then no other Greeks would dare to resist the Persians. So Leonidas led a mere 300 men, his personal bodyguards, to Thermopylae, while the rest of Sparta hesitated. He was reinforced by troops from a dozen other Greek cities, so his force eventually numbered 7,000.

Many in Athens believed that because they had provided the majority of the fleet, they should command the navy. It was at this pivotal moment that Themistocles conceded the command of the navy to the Spartans. The need for unity was more important than Athenian pride. The navy would be commanded by the Spartan Eurybiades. When some people in Athens protested to Themistocles, saying that the Spartans knew nothing about fighting at sea, Themistocles answered with a smile. "Then the Spartan admiral will not realize that it is really I who am in command!" Thus in the summer of 480 BC, the Greek forces took up their positions at Artemisium and Thermopylae. They did not have to wait long until Xerxes' army was upon them.

The Greek fleet at Artemisium consisted of 271 ships. Of these, by far the largest contingent was that of the Athenians, which numbered 127 ships. The Corinthians provided the second largest contingent of forty ships. The Spartans, who were in command, provided only ten. The Greeks soon received some favorable news. The Persian fleet, while anchored off the coast to the north, had been caught in a severe storm. So great was the size of the Persian navy that many ships had been forced to anchor out at sea. When the storm came up, many of these ships were destroyed. But the Persian fleet still held a great advantage in numbers.

The Greeks, upon hearing the news of the storm, took it as proof that the gods were on their side. However, when the Persian fleet came into view, panic set in. The Greeks doubted their ability to resist so great a navy. Eurybiades appeared uncertain about what to do. The people of Euboea, the island to the south of Artemisium, feared that the Greek navy would abandon them to the Persians, and they begged Eurybiades to stay. When this failed, they turned to Themistocles, to whom they gave a large sum of money. Keeping a part for himself, he passed the rest on to Eurybiades and the Corinthian admiral Adei-mantus, pretending the money was his own. This bribe convinced the admirals to fight at Artemisium. Once again, Themistocles showed that he was prepared to do anything to ensure that his policy prevailed. His strategy might have been unorthodox, but it was successful.

The Persians, seeing how few ships the Greeks possessed, were eager for battle. In order to destroy the Greek fleet once and for all, 200 ships were sent to sail around the island of Euboea and attack the Greek fleet from the south. Once encircled, none would escape. The Persians eagerly approached the Greeks, but in the narrow channel they could not bring their greater numbers to bear, and the battle proved inconclusive. The next day, the battle began anew, but soon news reached both sides that the Persian ships sailing around Euboea had been lost in another storm. Encouraged by this news, the Greeks fought well. For two more days the battle raged, with neither side gaining the upper hand. By the end of the third day, the Greeks were exhausted from battle, while the Persians were becoming increasingly demoralized. Even as the Greeks were debating whether to withdraw, a messenger arrived from Thermopylae.

While the navy was engaging the Persians at Artemisium, the army under the Spartan king Leonidas was facing the might of the Persian land forces. For two days, Leonidas's 7,000 men had held off vastly greater numbers

An artist's reconstruction of a scene from the sea battle at Salamis. The small inset reveals how Themistocles intentionally encouraged the Persians to surround the Greek fleet so that there was no escape and the Greek alliance had to fight.

of Persians. However, on the evening of the second day, a local shepherd appeared at Xerxes' camp and offered to show the Persians a little known mountain path that could be used to outflank the Greeks at Thermopylae. Xerxes dispatched his elite bodyguards, called the Immortals, to outflank the Greeks. Leonidas had discovered the existence of this path only upon his arrival at Thermopylae. He was able to spare only 1,000 men to guard it. These men failed to stop the Immortals, and in the early hours of the third day, Leonidas learned that he was soon to be surrounded. Thermopylae would fall to the Persians.

Realizing that any Greeks who remained to defend Thermopylae would die, Leonidas sent the majority of his army south. However, he understood that he could not go with them. If the Spartans were seen to flee at the first sign of a setback, it would reinforce the belief that the Persians could not be defeated. Then the fragile alliance would surely collapse and Greece, including Leonidas's beloved Sparta, would be enslaved. The only hope for the alliance was a symbolic last stand, a final act of defiance. Leonidas decided to remain with a handful of Spartans, along with the valiant volunteers from the city of Thespiae and the few Thebans who detested their own city's surrender to Persia. On the morning of the third day, Leonidas and 1,000 Greek warriors marched into battle, and into legend.

As the tale was recounted to the Greeks at Artemisium, their admiration for the bravery of Leonidas was overshadowed by fear that the fall of Thermopylae meant that all of central Greece was open to the Persians. Immediately, the Greek fleet withdrew, each contingent to its own city. As they sailed south, Themistocles left messages along the coast for the Ionian Greeks who were serving in Xerxes' navy. These men had been forced to serve the Persians, but Themistocles hoped they could be used to undermine Xerxes. The messages were placed at the natural harbors that the Persian fleet would have to use for shelter each night. Imploring the Ionians to remember that they were Greeks, Themistocles' messages urged them not to fight against their kinsmen. He knew that few Ionians would be able to desert Xerxes' army and join the Greeks. However, the messages would weigh heavily on their consciences and affect them in battle. And the Persians would become suspicious of them, questioning their loyalty. In this way

The Xerxes Gate at Persepolis

Themistocles sowed seeds of doubt and suspicion among the army of Xerxes. Yet the Persians, it seemed, were winning. With the death of Leonidas, Themistocles had lost his closest ally in Sparta. The Persian army was descending through Greece, burning and pillaging the towns and cities of all who had not submitted to them. As each moment passed, they came closer to Athens.

Plans had been drawn up for the evacuation of Athens, but few had believed that this would ever be necessary. Now it appeared there was no choice, and panic swept through the city. At the urging of Themistocles, the majority of the Athenian people began to depart from their homes. Most of the population went to the city of Troezen, on the coast of the Peloponnese. The young men went to the island of Salamis, where the fleet was gathering for a final stand against the Persians. Plutarch described the mournful scene, as the people left behind the old and the sick, who could not make the journey.

Another extreme measure was taken. Those ostracized by the Athenian people were to be recalled. These men still had popular followings in the city, and even their rivals admitted that the exiles were talented individuals. In the present crisis, every Athenian citizen would be called upon to help. A mere two years after his exile, Aristides returned to the city that had rejected him. Aristides and Themistocles would now have to work together.

Soon after the Athenians had deserted their city, Xerxes' army descended upon it. Despite heroic resistance, the few remaining defenders were eventually overpowered by the Persians, and all those still in Athens were slaughtered. The temples were burned to the ground, and the Athenians on Salamis could see the flames of their city flickering against the night sky. Xerxes had exacted his revenge for the sack of Sardis nearly twenty years before.

Yet Xerxes remained uncertain of his next move. Herodotus writes that Xerxes called a council of his commanders and asked them for advice. Most of them advised attacking the Greek fleet immediately. Only Artemisia, the queen of Halicarnassus in Asia Minor, advised differently. She warned Xerxes against any hasty action and suggested that he wait. Her logic was that the Greek alliance was fragile, and their supplies were low. As provisions ran out, the bickering between members of the alliance would increase, and the Greek navy would disperse like smoke in the morning breeze. Greece, she insisted, was almost in Xerxes' hands. Why risk a battle now? Xerxes was impressed with her council but impatient for victory. He decided to prepare for action as soon as possible.

Even as Athens burned, the commanders of the Greek fleet met to discuss where they should face the Persians. The fleet now numbered more than 370 ships, over half of which were Athenian, and they now had valuable experience fighting the Persians at sea. However, they were still heavily outnumbered. Word reached the admirals that the army had retreated to the Isthmus of Corinth, where a wall was being built to defend the Peloponnese. Since the death of Leonidas, no leading Spartan favored fighting to the north. The Peloponnesians in the fleet wanted to retreat to the isthmus and join the army. Salamis, they claimed, was a death trap. If the Persians defeated them there, they would have no safe place to which they could retreat. At the isthmus, they could retreat to their own cities in the Peloponnese. The only admiral who rejected this idea was Themistocles, who called on the others to reconsider. Adeimantus, the Corinthian admiral, interrupted him, saying that a man without a city should not lecture those who still possessed homes. This angered Themistocles, and he replied: "It is true, you wretch, that we gave up our homes. But we did so because we do not wish to be enslaved for things that have no soul. What we still possess is two hundred ships of war, themselves the greatest city in all Greece. And they are ready to defend *you.* Unless, of course, you decide to betray us, and all Greece, by fleeing from the enemy."

Then Themistocles turned to Eurybiades. He warned the Spartan that if they decided to fight at the isthmus, then the superior numbers of the Persian fleet would quickly crush them. However, in the narrows at Salamis, the Persians could not use their superior numbers, while the smaller Greek ships would be more effective. Moreover, he added, should the Peloponnesians decide to retreat now, then the Athenians would leave Greece altogether. They would take their fleet and build a new city in Italy, where they could live free from the danger of foreign invaders and the greater danger of faithless friends and cowardly allies. This threat unnerved Eurybiades. Much to the annoyance of the other admirals, Eurybiades ordered the fleet to remain at Salamis. Themistocles had, for the moment, won the day.

As the sun rose over Salamis, the Greeks saw the Persian fleet assembling, and they saw the Persian army gathering on the coastline. The size of the Persian forces terrified the Greeks, who once again began to consider retreating. Seeing that his argument was no longer convincing the admirals, Themistocles formed a new and daring plan to force the issue. Themistocles possessed a slave named Sicinnus, who, according to Herodotus, was quite devoted to his master. Themistocles secretly sent Sicinnus to Xerxes with a message. On reaching the Persian camp, Sicinnus was taken before Xerxes and repeated the message. "Themistocles of Athens has come over to the side of the Great King, and wishes to inform His Majesty that the Greek fleet is planning to retreat. He advises the King not to let them escape, but to attack them before they join their land forces. The Greeks are not united, and while they argue among themselves, they will be easy victims for Your Majesty."

This news delighted Xerxes. As at Thermopylae, he believed he had found a traitor to turn the tide in his favor. Immediately, he ordered the 200 ships of his Egyptian contingent to sail around the island of Salamis to prevent the escape of the Greek fleet. His scouts had noticed a small island, called Psyttaleia, at the entrance to the strait between Salamis and the mainland. The Greek fleet lay in this straight, soon to be trapped by his Egyptian ships. Sensing the strategic importance of this island, Xerxes ordered a large force of infantry to land on Psyttaleia. These soldiers would be able to rescue any Persian sailors who were ship-wrecked in the battle and capture any Greeks unfortunate enough to be washed ashore. The rest of his navy prepared to attack the Greeks.

The Greek admirals were still arguing about what course of action to take when news arrived that the Persians had blocked the west-ern passage between Salamis and the mainland. The first to bring this news was Aristides. Taking Themistocles aside, he faced his old adversary sternly and said, "We are not friends, Themistocles, but we should lay our hatreds aside. It is time for us to be rivals, not for our own sakes, but to see who can do the most good for Athens." Themistocles readily agreed and asked Aristides to take the news of the Persian encirclement to the other admirals himself, for if they heard it from Themistocles they would not believe it. Thus the two great rivals stood together, as they had done ten years before at Marathon. Soon Aristides' news was confirmed by deserters from the Persian fleet. The Greeks were trapped. They had no choice but to fight. Themistocles' secret message to Xerxes had achieved its purpose.

As the sun rose over the island of Salamis, the Persian fleet sailed out for battle. Xerxes had his throne set up on the cliffs that overlooked the strait and prepared to watch his fleet destroy the Greeks. Beneath his gaze, he counted the nations that called him their king. The news that the Greek commanders were not in agreement encouraged the Persians to expect an easy victory. Indeed, many of the Greeks, they hoped, would come over to the Persian side.

The poet Aeschylus recorded that the Persians could hear the Greeks before they could see them. In the early autumn, the dawn mist hung heavy over the Greek islands. As the forward ships of the Persian fleet sailed toward the mist-shrouded island, they expected little opposition. But then they heard the sound of voices raised in song: the rousing tones of the *paean*, or war hymn. As they peered into the mist, vague shapes became clear. Then from the dense banks of mist, the Greeks came forward, surging through the waves. With the Athenians came the Aeginetans, the Megarans, the Spartans, and ships from a dozen other Greek cities.

An artist's recon-
struction of Greek
triremes engaged in
ramming maneuvers

A detail from a vase painting showing Greek oarsmen

Themistocles had delayed his attack until the Persian fleet was well into the strait between Salamis and the mainland. He had also waited until the breeze from the open sea had blown through the strait, making the waters choppy and uneven. Then he sent his ships forward. The Greek ships, small and low in the water, were little affected by the breeze. However, the Persian ships, tall and heavy, were blown out of formation. In the choppy waters, they could not hold their line. The narrows allowed them little room to maneuver. In the breeze, many Persian ships turned sideways, leaving their wide hulls open to the Greek attack. As the Greeks rammed into the collapsing line of the enemy fleet, panic set in among the Persians. Some ships tried to turn back, but they only turned into the next advancing line of Persian ships. Confusion reigned, and the Persian ships rammed into one another. The Greeks, now descending from all sides, fell upon the Persians. Their smaller ships were more maneuverable in the narrow waters. From his vantage point above the battle, Xerxes watched in disbelief as his navy was destroyed before his eyes.

As the battle at sea turned in favor of the Greeks, Aristides led a small group of infantry to recapture the island of Psyttaleia. The Persians stationed on the island were massacred, and Aristides placed his men on the beaches to rescue shipwrecked Greek sailors. From there they watched as the remnants of the Persian fleet limped past them. As night fell in the narrow waters off Salamis, the Greek ships regrouped and returned to the island to prepare for the next attack. It never came.

The Greeks could sense that they had won a major victory. However, the enemy was not yet defeated, and they had lost more than forty ships themselves. For the time being, they

A vase painting of a Greek warship

hoped, they had command of the sea. But once the Persians regrouped, they would still be a formidable foe, and they still had control of the land.

To the Persians, the battle was a disaster. They lost some 200 ships, the cream of their navy. Xerxes, having witnessed the defeat, suddenly became afraid that he might be in danger. He feared what the Greeks would do if they captured him. Therefore, he decided to retreat

to Asia, leaving a part of his army in Greece.

Unaware of the Persian king's fears, the Greeks ventured out warily the next morning. The Persian fleet had already departed. Suddenly, the Greeks realized the extent of their success. A council of the admirals was called, and Themistocles suggested that they sail with all due speed to the Hellespont to destroy the bridge Xerxes had built there for his army three months earlier. Eurybiades and Aristides disagreed. Leave the bridge, they insisted, so that the Persians can flee back to Asia, and Greece will be rid of them. If the bridge was destroyed, the Persian army, with no way to retreat, would turn like a cornered rat and fight. Because of the army's size, they might still be victorious.

Since the other admirals agreed with Eurybiades and Aristides, Themistocles changed his mind. There was more to this than Themistocles would admit, however. Being

Hoplites marching into battle

known as the man who prevented the destruction of the Hellespont bridge, rather than the man who proposed its destruction, might serve him well in future dealings with the Persians. Themistocles was already thinking of what might occur after the war. To ensure that the Persians believed he was secretly on their side, Themistocles sent another message to Xerxes. Although the exact content of the message is unknown, Herodotus says that Themistocles told Xerxes that he himself had prevented the Greek navy from destroying the Hellespont bridge. Plutarch, however, claims that Themistocles warned Xerxes that the Greeks were *going* to destroy the bridge, and that as a friend to Xerxes, Themistocles was giving the Persians advance warning. Whatever the message said, it served two purposes. First, it

encouraged Xerxes to leave Greece as quickly as possible. Second, it made Xerxes think that Themistocles was his friend.

Thus, Xerxes decided to leave Greece. He took the larger part of his army with him, as well as the remnants of his navy. He prepared to portray his invasion of Greece as a success. The original target of his invasion, Athens, had been captured and destroyed. Moreover, he had faced and fought, if not defeated, the Greeks on land and sea, at Thermopylae and Artemisium. He claimed that he was needed back in Persia, for a king cannot leave his kingdom for too long. Xerxes left General Mardonius in Greece with a hand-picked force of nearly 100,000 men. The great king reasoned that these troops would surely be enough to subdue the Greeks. Xerxes, however, was going home.

For the Greeks, the enormity of their achievement was clear. The poet Aeschylus, who witnessed the battle himself, immortalized it in his play *The Persians*. Later, Herodotus, who spoke to many veterans of the engagement, recorded it for history. The Greeks, led by the Athenians, overcame an enemy who vastly outnumbered them and who had far greater experience of war at sea. After the battle, the Greek commanders divided the spoils. They gave rewards for courage to the men who had distinguished themselves in the battle. Above all, and in spite of the rivalries between the commanders, each man knew who was responsible for this remarkable victory— Themistocles of Athens.

There is little mention of Themistocles in the final stages of the war against the Persians. He led part of the fleet, and without the knowledge of the other admirals, he allegedly extorted money from some of the Greek islanders who had submitted to Xerxes. Upon his return to the mainland, he went to Sparta, where he was accorded honors never before given to an Athenian. He was presented with a crown of olives as a symbol of valor, was given a beautiful chariot, and received an escort of 300 elite Spartan warriors for part of his journey home.

The Persian forces under Mardonius spent the winter in Thessaly and returned to Attica the following spring. Once again the Athenians deserted their city, and Mardonius captured the empty city. At first he attempted to make peace with the Athenians and win them over to the Persian cause, but the Athenians rejected his entreaties. Instead, they turned to the Spartans for help. After much hesitation, the Spartans sent a force of 5,000 men north under the command of Pausanias. This army, reinforced by troops from many cities, including Athens, finally came face to face with the army of Mardonius in the summer of 479 BC, on the plains near the city of Plataea. There, the Greeks, spearheaded by the Spartans, routed the Persians, despite being outnumbered two to one. On the same day, the Greek fleet under the Spartan king Leotychidas inflicted a heavy defeat on the Persian navy at Mycale on the coast of Asia Minor. The Persian threat, for the time being, was eliminated.

RENEGADE OF ATHENS

Even as the victory celebrations continued, it was understood that the war was far from over. The battle would be taken to Persian soil to liberate the Greeks who lived under Persian rule in Asia and to punish the Persians for sacking so many Greek cities. The army of the alliance, under Pausanias of Sparta, was sent to continue the campaign against the enemy. Yet the Greek cities began to eye each other suspiciously once again.

In Athens, the work of rebuilding began. But even as the Athenians started to reconstruct the city walls, ambassadors arrived from Sparta ordering them to stop. Why, asked the Spartans, would Athens need to rebuild its walls? Surely the Greek cities were allies. Should the Persians invade again, a fortified Athens would merely provide a fortress for the enemy. The Spartans pointed to their own city, which had never been walled, saying that they preferred to place their trust in the strength of their arms rather than in cold stone. Themistocles could see their real motive, however. The Spartans, aware of the new role Athens was playing in international affairs, now saw her as a rival. A walled Athens would be much harder for the Spartans to control.

Themistocles traveled quickly to Sparta to insist that no such walls were being built. When the Spartans doubted him, he told them to send ambassadors to Athens to see for themselves. So confident was Themistocles that he told the Spartans to hold him hostage until the ambassadors returned. When the Spartan ambassadors reached Athens, they discovered the building work was well under way. As they tried to leave, the Athenians insisted that they remain until Themistocles was released by the Spartans. At last the Spartans realized they had been deceived. By the time Themistocles and the Spartan ambassadors were released, the walls of Athens were nearly complete. However, the Spartans were still well disposed toward Themistocles. They remembered the good he had brought Greece during the war, and they let the matter pass.

Yet the bickering continued. At a meeting of the Amphictionic League, a sacred Greek council that had existed for centuries, the Spartans insisted that all the cities that had joined the Persians should be expelled. Popular as this proved with many, Themistocles opposed it on behalf of Athens. If major states such as Thebes and Argos were excluded, the league could easily be controlled by Sparta. Fearing this, Themistocles convinced the delegates to reject the Spartan proposal. For a second time, Themistocles had confounded Spartan policy, and their patience with him began to wear thin.

Matters were turning against the Spartans. The allied Greek forces began to resent the arrogant way Pausanias treated them, and after many complaints, he was recalled to Sparta. The replacement commander proved no more popular, and the allies instead turned to Athens to lead them in the war against Persia. The Athenians eagerly agreed, and in 477 BC, an alliance was formed of all the states willing to continue the war. The agreement was officially signed on the island of Delos, and thus is called the Delian League by modern historians. The real force behind the alliance, however,

A painting on an amphora, a large storage jar, of young men racing

was Athens. Yet there was no place for Themistocles in the hierarchy of the league. Too many allies remembered his brutal extortion of the islanders after the Battle of Salamis. Aristides was appointed chief treasurer, while the young and charismatic Cimon was appointed one of its generals. Cimon, like Aristides, had little love for Themistocles. He was the son of Miltiades, the hero of Marathon, and remembered his father's rivalry with Themistocles from nearly twenty years earlier. Moreover, he was an aristocrat with a strong sympathy for Sparta, and he was unimpressed with Themistocles' anti-Spartan policies. The appointment of such bitter rivals to these prominent positions did not bode well for Themistocles.

The influence of Themistocles was on the wane. In Athens, his political rivals were beginning to overshadow him. Distressed by this, Themistocles constantly reminded the assembly of his achievements, which only served to alienate him further. Seeing their chance, his opponents plotted against him. Rumors were spread claiming that he desired to be tyrant, and his boastful attitude was seen to confirm this. At some point in the late 470s BC, Themistocles, the savior of Athens, was ostracized.

After his banishment, Themistocles settled in the city of Argos. Here he shunned any involvement in the city's politics. He was approached by Pausanias, the Spartan who had led the Greeks to victory at Plataea. Like Themistocles, Pausanias had found that the glory and respect he had earned in the war against Persia had been short-lived. After being recalled to Sparta, he found his ambitions frustrated. As a regent for the young son of Leonidas, he could never expect great power. And so he began to plot the overthrow of the Spartan government and even made contact with the Persians. Now, Pausanias hoped that Themistocles, also rejected by the people he had saved, would be will-ing to join the plot. But Themistocles rejected his offer. Out of respect for his old friend, though, he agreed to tell no one about the plot and assumed that Pausanias would soon abandon such a desperate and foolhardy project. But Pausanias continued his planning and was soon betrayed. Facing trial and execution, he fled to a temple that provided sanctuary to fugitives. Unable to arrest him on sacred ground, the Spartans surrounded the temple until Pausanias starved to death. In the investigation that followed, they found documents incriminating

A depiction of two Greek hoplites in charge of two captured enemy warriors

A painting of a man diving from a tower into a pool of water

Themistocles and revealing the offer Pausanias had made to him. Still angry at Themistocles for his anti-Spartan policies in the past, the Spartans sent ambassadors to Athens to demand his arrest and trial for treason. Shocked at the allegation, the Athenians dispatched officers with the Spartans to travel to Argos and arrest Themistocles.

However, a few people were still sympathetic to Themistocles, and he received word of the warrant for his arrest. Themistocles knew that many powerful people in both Athens and Sparta wanted to see him destroyed and that he was unlikely to be acquitted. He fled to the island of Corcyra near the western coast of Greece, and then to Epirus in northwestern Greece. While in Epirus, Themistocles had his family smuggled out of Athens to join him. His pursuers were still chasing him, and Themistocles knew that he could not remain in Epirus for long. He realized that there was only one place where he would be safe from the officers of Sparta and Athens. Themistocles, the hero of Salamis, fled to Persia.

Themistocles traveled across the Aegean Sea, where he almost sailed into the hands of the Athenian navy, and then took refuge with friends in Asia Minor. It was not until about 464 BC that he arrived in Susa, the capital of the Persian Empire. Xerxes, assassinated in 465 BC, had been succeeded by his son Artaxerxes. Themistocles presented himself to the new king. When questioned by a courtier of Artaxerxes, Themistocles impressed the Persian with his obvious intelligence but refused to reveal his identity. He insisted that no one in Persia would know who he was before the king. Accepting this, the courtier led Themistocles to the king.

As he entered the king's presence, Themistocles prostrated himself before Artaxerxes. This sign of submission was a custom of the Persians, but it was thought barbaric by the Greeks, who believed it was beneath the dignity of a free man to prostrate himself before another man. Themistocles was signaling his complete submission to the king. Artaxerxes turned to his interpreter and asked this stranger who he was. Plutarch records Themistocles' answer:

> O Great King, I am Themistocles of Athens, and have come to you as an exile, pursued by my own people. I brought many disasters upon the Persians, but

also many benefits, for it was I who prevented the Greeks from destroying the
army of your father. Once Greece was
safe, I warned him about our plans, so
that he could return home in safety. The
enmity my own people bear toward me,
and the accusations of treason, prove that
I have been a friend to Persia in the past.
Now I stand before you, and you may do
what you will with me. You can show your
grace and wisdom by saving me, and if
you choose to kill me it will only be an
enemy of the Greeks whom you destroy.

Artaxerxes remained silent and sent
Themistocles away. After Themistocles had
departed, the king celebrated his good fortune.
The man who had brought ruin to his father
and disgrace to all Persia was now in his hands.
That night, as Artaxerxes slept, he is said to
have called out three times: "I have
Themistocles of Athens!"

The following day, Artaxerxes called
together his advisers and had Themistocles
brought before them. Some among the king's
court remembered the tricks Themistocles had
played before and were highly suspicious of
his intentions. Artaxerxes, however, was

The remains of the Necropolis at Naqsh-I-Rustan, which contained the tombs of the Persian kings Darius, Xerxes, and Artaxerxes.

impressed, and said that the princely sum of 200 talents, which had been offered as a reward for Themistocles' capture, would now be given to him. Themistocles' foresight paid off. The man who had played the central role in defeating Xerxes' invasion of Greece was now welcomed in Persia as a friend. Artaxerxes knew that Themistocles would be a useful ally in his continuing war against the Greeks. The Persian king asked Themistocles to advise him on Greek affairs and promised him great rewards for his cooperation.

During the next few years, Themistocles became a great favorite of the king, whom he advised on many matters. Some members of the Persian court distrusted him, but they could not shake the king's confidence in his new friend. In return for Themistocles' services, Artaxerxes bestowed many gifts upon the Greek. He was made governor of the city of Magnesia in Asia Minor. His wealth was considerable. Yet Themistocles still missed Athens. In Persia, he had few friends. He once had a beautiful dining room built that could seat only nine guests and then stated that he would be happy indeed if he could ever fill it with friends. He remained an Athenian at heart.

Various stories are told about his death, and historians cannot determine which is true. Some allege that he simply died of sickness while in Magnesia. Plutarch records a different version. He claims that Artaxerxes, who was still fighting the Greeks, called upon Themistocles to help him in the war. Themistocles did not wish to tarnish the glory of his earlier achievements and found himself torn between his loyalty to his homeland and his gratitude to Artaxerxes. Thus, he decided to take his own life. Gathering his family and his few friends around him, he took each by the hand and wished them farewell, and then took poison. Far away from the land he had saved, Themistocles, the citizen, the general, and the renegade of Athens, died around 460 BC. His legacy was the successful defense of Greece at a time when its people had just begun the great experiment with democracy.

EPILOGUE

The people of Magnesia erected a great tomb for Themistocles. Some claim that his body was taken back to Attica and secretly buried there, while his tomb in Magnesia lay empty. The Athenians eventually forgave their hero and erected a monument in his honor, the remains of which can still be seen on the coast of the Piraeus.

Yet the greatest monument to Themistocles was not made of marble. In the wake of the Persian invasion, Athens had become the greatest city in Greece. Under a series of brilliant leaders—Aristides, Cimon, and Pericles—Athens entered a golden age. To this age belong the great temples of the Acropolis, including the Parthenon, buildings that have become the defining symbol of Western civilization. Art, literature, and philosophy flourished,

The ruins of the Apadana, the main audience hall of Darius I

and under Pericles, Athens embraced radical democracy, creating new definitions of freedom that would change the way people would think about themselves forever.

For the next fifty years, Athens would dominate Greece. But in the city's greatness lay the seeds of its destruction. The great freedoms that the citizens enjoyed were based on the brutal repression of slaves and allies. The Delian League slowly became an empire and the allies became subject states. In 449 BC, a peace treaty was signed with the Persians, but the Athenians continued to extort funds from their allies. Eventually, even Pericles conceded that the empire of Athens had become a tyranny. But by then it was too late. The Spartans were finally stirred into action and were seen as liberators of Greece from Athenian oppression. For thirty years, the two great cities, whose unity had once saved Greece from the Persians, fought each other. After a generation of bloodshed, Athens submitted.

The memory of Themistocles survived, but his faults were not forgotten. He had been vain and calculating, often intent on promoting himself as much as benefiting his people. He was the consummate politician. Yet he was also the savior of Greece. When danger had threatened, he had used all his skills as a politician to defend Greece. The life of Themistocles proves that, in some cases, the greatest heroes are not always the most virtuous people.

GLOSSARY

Aristides Athenian statesman, often called "the Just." Political rival of Themistocles, he was ostracized in 482 BC but recalled in 480 BC to play a major role in the war against Persia.

Artaxerxes Son of Persian king Xerxes, he succeeded his father in 464 BC.

Artemisia Queen of Halicarnassus in Asia Minor. As a subject ruler owing allegiance to Persia, she accompanied Xerxes' invasion of Greece in 480 BC.

Artemisium Peninsula on the north coast of the island of Euboea; site of a naval battle between the Greeks and Persians in August 480 BC.

Attica Region of Greece in which Athens was located.

Cleisthenes Athenian statesman who introduced in 507 BC the first democratic constitution.

Darius King of Persia from 521 to 486 BC. (In Persian, his name was Darayavaush.) Invaded Greece in 490 BC but was defeated at Marathon. Father of Xerxes.

Delian League Alliance formed in 477 BC to continue the war against Persia.

Delphi A city in central Greece; site of one of the most important religious centers in the ancient world. Greeks came here from all over the Mediterranean to consult the god Apollo and receive prophecies about the future.

Eurybiades Spartan admiral, commander-in-chief of the Greek forces at the Battles of Artemisium and Salamis.

Herodotus Historian and author of a history of the Persian wars. He is generally considered to be the first historian and has been called the "father of history." His epic work retells the events of the great war between the Greeks and the Persians. His work stands as our main source of information for the period.

Hipparchus Younger son of Peisistratus. Played an important role in the government of his brother Hippias. He was murdered in 514 BC in a personal dispute.

Hippias Son of Peisistratus. Tyrant of Athens from 527 BC until he was driven out in 510 BC.

hoplite Heavily armored infantryman who served as the backbone of the Greek armies. Each man wore a heavy bronze breastplate and helmet and carried a large round shield made of bronze called a *hoplon*. At his side he carried a short sword, but his main weapon was a spear about nine feet long. The hoplites fought in what is known as a *phalanx*. This was a tightly packed formation of men, designed to be impenetrable. From the front, the enemy would see only a wall of bronze shields. The real strength of the phalanx was the sense of unity it created among the hoplites. Because the shield was always carried on the left arm, it protected only the left side of the man who carried it. His right side would be protected by the shield of the man to his right, while his own shield was protecting the man to his left. Thus each man was actually protected by someone else's shield. The phalanx could work only when each man was prepared to trust his neighbor with his life. If a man dropped his shield, the first man to die would be his neighbor, and this responsibility gave men extra courage.

Immortals The elite soldiers of the Persian army and the personal bodyguards of the king.

Leonidas King of Sparta from 490 to 480 BC. Greek commander at Thermopylae.

Leotychidas King of Sparta from 491 to 469 BC. Commanded Greek forces at the Battle of Mycale in 479 BC.

Marathon A broad plain twenty-six miles northeast of Athens; site of the famous victory over the Persians in 490 BC.

Mardonius Persian general. Commanded the Persian forces at the Battle of Plataea in 479 BC.

Pausanias Regent of Sparta. Commanded Greek forces at the Battle of Plataea in 479 BC.

Peisistratus Tyrant of Athens from 561 BC to 527 BC. Father of Hippias and Hipparchus.

Plataea City in central Greece, ally of the Athenians at Marathon; site of the Greek victory over the Persians in 479 BC.

Plutarch Historian who lived from 50 AD to 120 AD. One of the most important sources for the history of ancient Greece.

polis (poleis) The form of city-state found in ancient Greece.

Salamis Island near Athens; site of the Greek naval victory over the Persians in 480 BC.

Solon Athenian leader who introduced a series of reforms in the early sixth century BC.

Thebes Major city in central Greece; supported the Persians in 480 BC.

Thermopylae The only road through the mountains from northern to central Greece lay along the coast at Thermopylae. It was here that Leonidas and his army faced the Persians in 480 BC.

Thespiae City in central Greece; Thespian soldiers volunteered to stay with Leonidas at Thermopylae.

Trireme Greek warship, with three rows of oars on each side.

Xerxes King of Persia from 485 to 465 BC. Invaded Greece in 480 BC with a vast army. Son of Darius. He was assassinated in 465 BC.

FOR MORE INFORMATION

American Classical League
Miami University
Oxford, OH 45056
e-mail: info@aclclassics.org
Web site: http://www.aclclassics.org

The Classical Association
Room 323, Third Floor
Senate House
London WC1E 7HU
England
020-7862-8706
e-mail: Clare.Roberts@sas.ac.uk
Web site: http://www.sas.ac.uk/icls/
   classass

International Plutarch Society
Department of History
Utah State University
0710 Old Main Hill
Logan, UT 84322-0710
Web site: http://www.usu.edu/
   history/plout.htm

National Junior Classical League
Miami University
Oxford, OH 45056-1694
(513) 529-7741
Web site: http://www.njcl.org

WEB SITES
Due to the changing nature of Internet links, the Rosen Publishing Group, Inc., has developed an online list of Web sites related to the subject of this book. This site is updated regularly. Please use this link to access the list:

http://www.rosenlinks.com/lag/them/

FOR FURTHER READING

Bradford, Ernle. *The Year of Thermopylae.* London: Macmillan, 1980.

Cassin-Scott, Jack. *The Greek and Persian Wars* (Osprey Men at Arms Series No. 69). London: Osprey, 1977.

Hanson, Victor Davis. *The Wars of the Ancient Greeks* London: Cassell, 1999.

Herodotus. *The Histories.* Translated by Aubery de Sélincourt. London: Penguin, 1972.

Plutarch. "The Life of Themistocles" in *The Rise and Fall of Athens.* Translated by Ian Scott-Kilvert. London: Penguin, 1960.

BIBLIOGRAPHY

Aeschylus. *The Persians* in *Prometheus Unbound and Other Plays.* Translated by Philip Vellacott. London: Penguin, 1961.

Burn, Andrew R. *Persia and the Greeks.* London: Duckworth, 1984.

Green, Peter. *The Greco-Persian Wars.* Berkeley: University of California Press, 1996.
(Originally published as *The Year of Salamis.* London: Weidenfeld & Nicolson, 1970.)

Herodotus. *Historiae.* Edited by Charles Hude. Oxford: Clarendon Press, 1908.

Herodotus. *Histories.* Translated by A. D. Godley. Loeb Classical Library. Cambridge, MA: Harvard University Press, 1926.

Hignett, Charles. *Xerxes' Invasion of Greece.* Oxford: Clarendon Press, 1963.

Jones, A. H. M. *Athenian Democracy.* New York: Johns Hopkins University Press, 1986.

Lazenby, John. *The Defence of Greece.* Warminster, England: Aris & Phillips, 1993.

Lenardon, Robert. *The Saga of Themistocles*. London: Thames and Hudson, 1978.

Morrison, J., J. Coates, and N. Rankov. *The Athenian Trireme: The History and Reconstruction of an Ancient Greek Warship*. Cambridge, England: Cambridge University Press, 2000.

Plutarch. "Aristides" in *Plutarch's Lives, volume 2*. Translated by Bernardotte Perrin. London: Loeb Classical Library, 1914.

Plutarch. "Themistocles" in *Plutarch's Lives, volume 2*. Translated by Bernardotte Perrin. London: Loeb Classical Library, 1914.

Poldecki, Anthony J. *The Life of Themistocles*. Montreal: McGill-Queen's University Press, 1975.

Todd, S. *Athens & Sparta*. London: Duckworth, 1996.

INDEX

ABOUT THE AUTHOR

Ian Macgregor Morris was born in 1971 to a Scottish father and Dutch mother, and spent much of his early life traveling between Britain and the Netherlands. Educated at Rugby School, he went on to earn his B.A. at University College London and his Ph.D. at the University of Manchester. He has worked extensively on ancient and modern history, carried out archaeological fieldwork in Greece, and worked on television documentaries on Greek history. He is currently an Honorary University Fellow in the Department of Classics and Ancient History, University of Exeter.

CREDITS